Dividend Investing

Proven Strategies for Creating Massive Wealth with Dividend Stocks

James Willick

© Copyright 2019 - All rights reserved.

The content contained within this book may not be reproduced, duplicated or transmitted without direct written permission from the author or the publisher.

Under no circumstances will any blame or legal responsibility be held against the publisher, or author, for any damages, reparation, or monetary loss due to the information contained within this book. Either directly or indirectly.

Legal Notice:

This book is copyright protected. This book is only for personal use. You cannot amend, distribute, sell, use, quote or paraphrase any part, or the content within this book, without the consent of the author or publisher.

Disclaimer Notice:

Please note the information contained within this document is for educational and entertainment purposes only. All effort has been executed to present accurate, up to date, and reliable, complete information. No warranties of any kind are declared or implied. Readers acknowledge that the author is not engaging in the rendering of legal, financial, medical or professional advice. The content within this book has been derived from various sources. Please consult a licensed professional before attempting any techniques outlined in this book.

By reading this document, the reader agrees that under no circumstances is the author responsible for any losses, direct or indirect, which are incurred as a result of the use of information contained within this document, including, but not limited to, — errors, omissions, or inaccuracies.

Table of Contents

Table of Contents iv

Introduction 7

What Are Dividends? 11

   Why Companies Pay Them? 13

   What Are the Advantages of Dividend Investing? 17

      Safety 18

      Payments Go Up 23

      Uncomplicated Withdrawal when Renting 25

      Multiple Ways to Make Profit 26

      More Likely to Make Profit in Unsettling Times 27

The Harsh Truth: Long-Term Investments 31

   Inflation 33

   Taxes 36

   Fees 38

   The Long-Term Worth 40

The Fundamental Rules of Dividend Investing 43

   Quality 44

Long-Term Thinking 45

How to Pick Stocks 49

What Is a "Quality" Company? 50

The Step by Step Process to Choosing the Right Stock .. 54

The Main Ratios to Calculate 57

   1. The Dividend Payout Ratio 58

   2. The Dividend Coverage Ratio 58

   3. The Free Cash Flow to Equity Ratio 59

   4. The Net Debt to EBITDA Ratio 59

   The Dividend Growth 60

The Main Types of Dividend Stocks 63

ADRs 64

MLPs 66

REITs 69

Stock Selection Strategies and Building a Portfolio 71

ETF 72

DRIP 77

Dividend Capture Strategy 79

Dogs of the Dow 83

Protecting Your Investments 87

    Diversifying 88

        Variety over Quantity 89

        Split Your Money Correctly 90

    Are They Still Paying a Dividend? 93

    Keep Your Ears Open 96

    Stop Losses 98

The Most Common Mistakes to Avoid 101

    Chasing High Yields 102

    Starting When You're Old 104

    Getting Bored 108

    Following the Crowd 110

Conclusion 113

Leave a review 117

Introduction

It's hard not to be fascinated by the glamorous world of Wall Street when so many good movies portray it as this fast-moving, electric environment where big ideas (and big money) are made every minute.

If speedy transactions, people yelling to SELL, and luxurious yacht Saturdays infused with expensive alcohol and designer flip-flops are what you are looking for, I am sorry to be the one breaking the bad news to you: this book is not about that.

Sure, it could be. But definitely not next week, next month, or even next decade.

This book is about dividend investing: a type of stock investment that is intrinsically *slow*, and, to be terribly frank, quite boring in patches.

Why would anyone continue reading?

Because this book and dividend investing are about the attainable, down to earth goals - such as sending your kid off to a good college and offering him/her the chance to live a better life or simply living a good life yourself once you retire. It can be about a dream cruise vacation around the world or making sure you'll have a roof over your head once you reach retirement age. It could be about the aforementioned designer flip-flops, or it could be about being able to retire as early as possible and write the book you always wanted to write.

Dividend investing is not even by far as shiny and extravagant as other types of investment - but it is a far more stable, far more attainable, far closer to home strategy you can employ to fuel your dreams for the future.

My main goal with this book is to help you understand what dividend investing is and what are the basic concepts behind it that will help you build an investment portfolio that is profitable and safe at the same time.

We will navigate through the essentials of dividends and how they work and stop just for a minute to have coffee with their pros and cons. Then, we will get more familiar with the two governing rules of successful dividend investing.

And once that introductory part is done, we will jump right into the blue waters of *how to make the right choice* and *how to protect that choice*.

I hope this book will be an adventure for you - not an adventure of pirates and surprising gold nuggets, but an adventure of discovery and self-discovery. More than anything, dividend investing is all about playing it smart and safe, rather than aiming for the short, stormy gains.

More than that, I hope this book will eventually help you to build the future you and your family deserve: a luminous, comfortable future that makes you smile and be grateful every day.

What Are Dividends?

Dividend investments are one of the most popular types of investments. As you will see later on, there are multiple advantages that make this kind of investment a preferred one for a wide range of people.

Put simply: dividends are payments corporations make to their shareholders. Most often, this happens as a distribution of profits. The process is easy to understand; when a company is profitable, they will reinvest the profit in the business, and pay a part of the profit to their shareholders, as dividends.

To put this in perspective, consider the fact that "dividends" comes from the Latin "to divide" - so, they can be understood by the splitting or division of the profits among the shareholders, according to the number of stocks they hold in the company.

The payments made to the shareholders can be in cash (via bank account deposits) or by issuing further shares (if the company has a dividend reinvestment plan). When the dividends are paid, those who receive the payments (the investors) have to pay income tax. Moreover, the company making the payments will not receive a tax deduction for these payments.

Every dividend has a fixed amount on it. The more shareholding power you have in a company, the larger the dividend will be. Most of the public companies have a fixed schedule on how they pay these dividends, but they can still create special dividends to make an extra payment.

Cooperatives do not make fixed payments, but they allocate the dividends based on the activity of the members. Thus, most of the times, these are considered to be a pre-tax expense.

Why Companies Pay Them?

When businesses reach a certain level of maturity, they do not need to invest as much in themselves - and that is the moment they may consider issuing dividends.

One of the reasons they might want to do this is because a lot of investors are attracted by the idea of a steady income (which is what dividends can provide). Therefore, they will be more interested in buying a company's stock if the company is growing and thriving. On the other side of the fence, the company will be more likely to attract funds via dividend investments.

It is worth noting that the more desirable a company is, the higher the price of the dividend will be. For instance, some of the most well-known companies to offer dividend investment options include Apple, Microsoft, Verizon, and so on. Apple's stock price is of $207 at the moment[1], and if we consider a company in the same tech spectrum, but with much smaller desirability, Twitter's stock price is $39. [2]

---

[1] https://www.marketwatch.com/investing/stock/aapl
[2] https://www.marketwatch.com/investing/stock/twtr

Alright, a lot of companies sell stock - but not all of them pay dividends. There are a few reasons that might lead a company to do this:

- If a company is growing at a rapid pace, they will most likely not pay dividends because they want to reinvest their profits into further growth.
- Sometimes, even if a company is already mature, they might take the decision not to pay dividends because reinvesting in new assets or buying other companies are better for the long-term growth of the business.
- Sometimes, companies might be considering the expenses of issuing new stock - and thus, they might choose to reinvest their earnings, as opposed to issuing dividends.

Not paying dividends may not sound like an advantage for an investor. However, it can be more beneficial for them if you look at the matter from a tax perspective. In this case, investors can pay as low as 0% and as high as 20% in terms of taxes (as opposed to paying 37% when dividends are paid normally).

Some examples of companies that have not paid dividends include Facebook, Amazon, and Tesla.

If, on the other hand, a business has excess earnings and takes the decision to pay dividends to their common shareholders, they will declare an amount, as well as a payable date. Most often, this happens quarterly, when the company has already finalized its income statement.

As mentioned before, dividends can be paid either as a dividend check or in additional shares of stock. Regardless of which of the options a company may settle for, it is worth noting that dividends are taxable income.

The first option is the most common and standard one. In this case, the shareholders receive a check by mail. Most often, this happens a few days after the ex-dividend date (which is the date when stock will start trading without considering the dividend that was previously declared).

When companies opt to pay dividends in the form of additional stock, they do so by abiding by their dividend reinvestment plan (DRIP). This type of plan can be quite advantageous for investors. For instance, if the investor wants to add to his/her equity holdings without further investment per se, a dividend reinvestment plan will make this process easier. Furthermore, DRIPs tend to be commission-free, since a broker does not have to be used in the process. This makes DRIP options quite appealing particularly to smaller investors who may not want to pay commission for smaller purchases of stock.

Furthermore, DRIPs are beneficial from the point of view of the price of the actual stock as well. Many times, companies offering such plans will offer the additional shares for sale at a discount. Combined with the lack of commission, this can lead to important savings for investors.

When a dividend is declared, all the shareholders will be announced through a press release. Moreover, the information will be shared with various stock quoting services as well.

When the declaration is made, a record date will be set. This means that all the shareholders who are on record by that date will be entitled to receive the payment. The ex-date is consisted of the day following the record date. Anyone who purchases shares on an ex-date will not be entitled to receive the dividends. The payments will be released to eligible shareholders approximately one month after the record date.

When the payable date arrives, the company will disburse the funds using a Depository Trust Company (DTC), sending the payments to the brokerage companies around the world that hold the shareholders' stock. These brokerage firms will apply the cash dividends to the eligible client accounts, or they will proceed with reinvesting the cash dividends according to the client's instructions.

What Are the Advantages of Dividend Investing?

Obviously, if dividend investing is so popular, it must pose some pretty big advantages, right?

Well, yes. Dividend investing does show considerable benefits that make this more popular than other types of investment.

Following, we will discuss some of the features that make dividend investments such a good option for such a wide range of investors.

Safety

Of course, one of the first things you will think about when creating an investment portfolio is whether or not it is safe - and when it comes to this, dividend investing is one of the safest baskets to put your eggs in.

Sure, you still have to make sure to not put *all* your eggs in the same basket (and definitely not in the same company when buying stock). But even so, dividend investment makes for a sane, fairly predictable type of investment.

When buying stock, most people think of their shares as an option to grow their portfolio - and this makes all the sense in the world. However, you should also consider at least part of your stock as an attractive alternative when it comes to generating actual, current income. The higher dividend-paying stocks in your portfolio can become a very important part of your safety plan for the future.

Aside from the fact that you get to see your money sooner, rather than later, in the form of dividend payments, you should also consider the fact that stocks are one of the easiest types of investments in terms of how you can grow them. Even when you *do* focus on a safe, income-generating portfolio, you should still include some stock options that have the potential to grow, because capital appreciation is desirable.

It is more than important to mention that not all dividend investment is safe - but using the right strategies and keeping your mind cool can help you create a portfolio that is safe, gives high returns back, and is as diverse as possible. To understand why dividend investing is a safe option, consider the following points:

1. Reinvested dividends are actually one of the largest parts of the total stock market. The cumulative return of the S&P 500 since the late 80s has been of no less than 431%.[3] If you take dividends out of the statistics, however, the cumulative total return drops to just 258%, showing just what an important role dividend investing plays on the market.

2. Dividends change over time, according to how profitable a company becomes (or how much its profitability drops). Depending on these changes, investors tend to change their focus to current income (from capital appreciation).

---

[3] https://dqydj.com/sp-500-return-calculator/

That doesn't sound like dividend investing is a safe option. However, certain types of stocks are known to have paid large dividends over the course of the years. In general, these are large and well-established companies. This means that as an investor, you should probably focus on older and more established indexes, such as the S&P 500 when looking for dividend investment options, rather than newer indexes, such as Russell 2000.

Furthermore, it is also worth noting that most of the new, rapidly growing industries (and the companies pertaining to them) are known to pay low dividends (or none at all, for that matter). This includes tech, biotech, and other similar companies. So, if you are looking for dividend investment options with high returns, you should probably look into the more traditional, slower-growing industries - such as drug companies, utility companies, and so on.

3. One of the safest dividend options are the broad-based indexes of stocks. These stocks allow for a lot more diversity than individual stocks and thus reduce the risks that come with holding a single stock that

doesn't perform well. High dividends usually come from mature companies that are already established on the market and show consistent earnings. More often than not, these companies' stock will not be very volatile, so they are not always the best option for stock investment for capital appreciation.

It is also worth noting that bonds and certificates of deposit are safer than most of the investment options, including dividend investing. The reason they are so safe is because their coupon payments are guaranteed by contract, while dividends are paid based on the company's discretion.

A lot of businesses pay dividends consistently and are committed to this, but this is not guaranteed by any kind of contract, so changes can occur. For example, if a business finds itself in financial difficulty or if the economy is poor, this might affect whether or not that business pays its dividends. The reason they do this is that they want to strengthen up their balance sheets, and not paying a dividend to the shareholders is one of the best ways to ensure that. Therefore, when investing in dividends, you should make sure to factor this risk and the impact it could have on your finances.

4. Preferred stocks are an option you might want to consider as well. This type of stocks stands between common stocks and bonds in terms of how companies structure their capital. Corporate bonds tend to be safer than preferred stocks, but even so, the latter is safer than common stocks.

   In general, preferred stocks don't offer a lot of room in terms of capital appreciation (or at least not as much as common stocks), but the current income is usually a compensation that makes them attractive to investors. Also, preferred stockholders are paid before the common stockholders, which means these types of stocks are more stable than the common ones.

   It is also important to know that companies can withhold preferred stock dividends if they are going through difficult times. So, the income from a preferred stock is less safe than that of a company bond.

Payments Go Up

Another feature that makes dividend investing appealing to investors is the fact that payments can go up. Of course, it is extremely important to note the fact that not *all* dividend stocks will grow over time - but when you select the right ones, this can be a considerable advantage.

There are three major elements to consider when selecting dividends that show the potential to grow:

1. The history of the dividends paid by that company. Look at what are the dividends currently paid by a company, as well as the way they have evolved historically. Be careful with companies that pay dividends that are too high, because these are usually associated with high risk as well (it is unsustainable for a business to pay this much in terms of dividends).

    The older a company is, the more history you will have to look at - and this is one of the very important reasons to invest in older companies when it comes to dividends. When you have a lot more to look at, you can go a bit further than guesswork and analyze a clear pattern for that company's dividend-paying behaviors. Yes, the performance of a company is not always a good indicator of how it will perform in the future, but even so, it is a very good point to start with when analyzing your investment options.

2. The valuation of the stock. When you want to select dividend investment options that have the potential to grow over time, you should look at the value of the stock you want to buy and make sure that it is the best possible price. For instance, when the stock markets crash, some investors take the opportunity and buy stock at a very low price. This is not something you should do if you are new in the art of investments, but it is something that *can* be done, provided that you have the data and the intel that the market will soon come back up.

Furthermore, you should also calculate the price/earnings ratio (divide the price of the stock at the moment by the earnings you will receive for every share in that company). This will not only help you determine how much your payments will be if nothing changes for the company, but it will also help you determine if that company's stock is undervalued or overvalued.

3. The quality of the stock. When analyzing dividend investing options, it is also quite important to look at the qualitative values of the company you are scrutinizing. In general, the more boring a company is, the better it will be for you (e.g., a company that was founded a long time ago, maybe even a century ago, and has very diverse activities all over the world). General Electric is a very good example in this sense - they might not come up with anything exciting, but they are very stable on the market, and they have been so for a long, long time.

   Furthermore, industries that show constant growth are also a good place to look at. For example, the healthcare and telecommunications industries are generally believed to grow at a steady pace, as the demand is constantly growing as well.

Uncomplicated Withdrawal when Renting

Dividend investing offers the option of renting stocks as well. This works a lot like renting an apartment: you pay a certain sum of money, and that place is yours to use for a given amount of time. On the other side, the person you are renting the apartment from gets to see immediate payments from an investment they made (buying real estate).

If you own stock, you can write a call option on the stock - which is similar to renting your apartment or house. Another investor will buy the call option from you, and the money they pay is deposited in your trading account. You cannot withdraw the money until the call option expires or the stock is sold - but given that call options are made for a predetermined amount of time (just like in the case of renting an apartment), it is easier for you to withdraw money than by selling the stock yourself.

Multiple Ways to Make Profit

Another advantage of using dividend investing in solidifying your portfolio is the fact that it will allow you to make money two ways. On the one hand, dividend investing can yield considerable profits if you invest in stocks that will appreciate in price. On the other hand, if the price does not appreciate, or if you simply decide not to sell your stock, you can still make a profit by receiving dividend payments.

Furthermore, when you collect dividend payments, you continue to be the owner of the stock, which means that its value will not instantly vanish from your portfolio. As mentioned before, dividend investing works best when you find old, well-established companies that offer such plans - so your investment will be there next year, and the year after that, and the year after that, until you decide to sell the shares.

Last, but not least, it is also important to keep in mind that dividend investing will provide you with the relatively quick cash you can use to grow your investment portfolio even more.

More Likely to Make Profit in Unsettling Times

As it was mentioned before, it is up to a company whether or not they pay their dividends. However, when it comes to bear markets (markets where shares are either dropping or flattening), companies that have historically paid dividends are more likely to continue paying them as long as their profitability is running well.

Again, it is entirely up to a company if they decide to pay their dividends or not - and they are most definitely not bound to doing this. Respectable companies with a lot of experience behind them are more likely to continue paying dividends, but it is not a *must* - so take this advantage with a pinch of salt.

Of course, these are just some of the basic, high-level advantages of dividend investing. it is extremely important to be aware of the fact that there is no perfect form of investing - each of them has upsides and downsides, and the key lies in creating a portfolio that allows you to continue making a profit even if one of the elements in it is not as profitable as it should be.

I will dedicate the following chapter to showing you how dividend investing can show significant disadvantages as well. This is crucial for your understanding of how dividend investing works. It is absolutely essential that you know what you are getting yourself into, both with its positives and with its negatives - the first will help you keep your eyes on the prize, while the latter will help you make sure you avoid major mistakes along the road.

Dividend Investing

As you will see, the major disadvantages of dividend investing are mostly connected to external factors, as well as how dividend investing is perceived at tax-level. Dividend investing is not in any way perfect - but balancing its pros and cons will help you get the bird's eye view and know exactly how to proceed when building your portfolio and including dividends in it.

The Harsh Truth: Long-Term Investments

There's an old saying: if something is too good to be true, it probably isn't.

The saying applies to investments as well: if you are ever advertised or sold an investment option that shows zero risks and yields excellent profits, you should think twice (and even three times, if necessary).

Nothing ever is perfect and investing makes no exception from the rule. "THIS trick brought them $5,000 in just ONE day"-type-of-ads are nothing but scams (at their very worst) or mere click-baits (at their very least).

Dividend investing is not a scam - it is a legit method to improve your portfolio and create long-term incomes you can live off. Most often, investors focusing on their retirement include dividends in their portfolio precisely because it helps them see more profit and live comfortably once retired.

This is not to say that dividend investing comes with no risks at all, or that it is absolutely perfect. On the contrary: I would be lying to say it was anything like this, and it wouldn't be fair to you, to this industry, for that matter.

This chapter is all about the harsh truth: the facts you have to face when investing in dividends because, well, they are what they are and being familiar with them will help you make the right decisions.

There are four main verticals you should consider when analyzing the disadvantages of dividend investing: inflation, taxes, fees, and the overall long-term worth. They will all be discussed in more detail below - so, by the end of this chapter, you will have the basic information to help you decide where investing in dividends will fit into your general investment strategy.

Inflation

Inflation is one of those financial terms people tend to overcomplicate when trying to explain it. However, it all boils down to one simple definition: inflation is on the rise when the price of goods is raised, and, consequently, each unit of currency loses a part of its buying power. So, in other words, if $10 bought a meal for four in the 1960s, it barely covers for a fast food meal for one person in 2019 - which means that inflation has grown over the past (nearly) six decades.

Inflation growth usually generates a snowball effect: the higher the price of goods is, the fewer people will buy, and thus, the revenues and the profits of a business will decline. As a result of this, the economy itself might slow down.

Historically, hyperinflation has had a major effect on different countries' economies. For example, it is said that in the 1920s it took an entire cart of money to buy a loaf of bread in Germany.

In more modern days, Venezuela's economy has drastically been affected by the rise of inflation. The country has been struggling for the last five years, and the situation has gotten so bad that people pay for fruit in *boxes* full of money. Although Venezuelans earn by the millions in national currency, this only translates to a few US dollars a month. Consequently, most stores are empty-shelved, and products are scarcely available. Even when products (like food and medicine) do exist on the market, they are extremely high-priced, which sends the entire economy down a spiral of decay. [4]

In the more stable markets, hyperinflation like this is unlikely to happen (but not completely impossible, given the "right" circumstances). In the US, the federal government keeps a close eye on signs that might show unexpected boosts in inflation, as this type of growth can be extremely painful because it usually affects companies across multiple quarters.

While consumers can see the effects of rising inflation quite quickly (they are simply unable to purchase the same

---

[4] https://www.theguardian.com/world/2018/jul/25/venezuela-inflation-crisis-nicolas-maduro

amount of goods with the same amount of money as they did before), things can be a little more confusing for investors because the effects of inflation are not that immediate when it comes to stock prices.

High inflation might be able to stimulate job growth under certain circumstances - but even so, it will still have a big impact on corporate profit, because of the higher input costs. When this happens, corporations might be more inclined to save money for the future and reduce (or completely eliminate) their dividend payments.

Inflation can affect both growth and value stock. Growth stock is characterized by a small current value, but with great potential of increasing over time. Value stock, on the other hand, shows a strong cash flow at the moment of purchase, but predictions point towards a decrease in value over time.

When high inflation influences interest rates, this will affect growth stocks more than it will influence value stocks. This does not mean that the latter will not be affected at all - but they will be influenced to a lesser extent.

Income generating stocks can definitely be affected by rising inflation. When inflation is on the rise, the purchasing power drops. In most of these cases, dividend payments do not coordinate well with the inflation levels. Consequently, income-generating stocks can appear less attractive to investors than in times of low inflation. Even more, although every dollar received on dividend payments will buy fewer goods, the taxes on these payments will stay the same, causing a double-negative effect of inflation over dividend investing.

At the same time, if you are looking to buy more stock in a company and you are waiting for the right moment and the right price, you should pay attention to inflation growth because these are among the times most likely to push down the price of stock.

Taxes

It is said that two things in life have absolute certainty: death and taxes.

When you are an investor, you have to be double-careful about your taxes, because each type of investment in your portfolio might be taxed differently.

Dividend Investing

Unfortunately, taxes are not one of the strong points of dividend investing. In fact, this type of investment is disadvantageous from two tax-related points of view.

The first one is connected to the fact that you will be double-taxed: once through the corporation tax applied to all the earnings made by a company (which will consequently lower the amount of money available for dividend payments) and the second time when you have to pay income tax on your received dividend payments.

Tax rates vary a lot from one investor to another, according to everyone's specific situation. In some cases, you might be able to legally reduce the taxes paid on dividends by using the so-called "tax-sheltered accounts" (IRAs, Roth IRAs, 401k accounts, and so on). It is, however, very important to discuss this with an accountant and see if this is your particular situation.

Furthermore, it is important to note that if a company does not pay its retained earnings in the form of dividends, they still have the option to buy back the shares you purchased from them. In this case, you might be better off selling the stock back than receiving dividends, because this way, you will not be paying as much in taxes. Again, however, this varies from one situation to another, so it is not a generally accepted rule of any kind.

The second tax-related disadvantage of owning dividend-paying stocks is connected to the fact that sometimes, these companies will tap investors. This usually happens when they need to raise cash (or when they want to raise fresh equity). When this happens, you might find yourself in a circling situation that makes you receive a dividend payment, and then you are asked by the company to pay cash in a rights issue. Consequently, you send the cash back to the company for further reinvestment, but you are faced with a tax wedge that is completely unnecessary.

Fees

Dividend-paying stocks are frequently associated with exchange-traded funds (also called ETFs). These funds collect the dividend payments on behalf of the investors, and then disburse them accordingly.

There are several disadvantages associated with this practice. On the one hand, these funds handle all the organizational matters of your investments, making it relatively easy for you to manage your portfolio.

On the other hand, this also means that ETFs will charge a fee for their services (which is normal, but not necessarily less annoying for investors who want to see higher profitability for their investments.

Furthermore, the timing of a dividend payment that goes through an EFT first might be delayed as well. Depending on the ex-dividend date, on the record date, and on the payment date set by the ETF you may or may not receive your dividend payments.

Different ETFs have different rules and fees, so it is quite important for you to analyze the ETF both from the point of view of the type of companies in it and from the point of view of the expense ratio (which shouldn't be higher than 0.50%).

Fees are quite unavoidable when it comes to dividend investing, but some ETFs might be better than others, for different people. This is why it is extremely important that you run an analysis that suits your particular situation and that you don't buy stock in a dividend-paying company just because you "heard" it's a good move.

The Long-Term Worth

Clearly, dividend investing shows a pretty good array of benefits. As mentioned before, one of the most important ones is the fact that this type of investment is frequently safer than others.

Unfortunately, "safe" is usually at the other end of the pole with "skyrocketing" - so you shouldn't expect your income to simply boom as a result of making dividend investments. Yes, they can definitely add to your portfolio, and yes, a collection of good dividend investment options can definitely help you boost your income.

However, you should not expect *The Wolf of Wall Street*-type of income growth.

Most of the dividends hold at about 2-3% in terms of yield. This means that if you invest $250,000, you will only see a maximum of $7,500 in dividend payments every year.

If your investment goal is retirement, that might amount to a considerable sum of money over the course of a couple of decades. However, it is important to know that the safest way to withdraw your investment money for retirement includes not touching the principal (the main investment you made).

Dividend Investing

If patience is your strong suit and you are using dividend investing in combination with other types of investment, the situation is far different, and dividends are a very good choice. Yet, if you are in a rush to make a fortune, this might not be the best solution for you.

Dividend investing is by no means an easy way out of financial worries. But then again, nothing is, except winning the lottery or accidentally striking a gold mine and buying a low-priced stock that will storm into a very good sale in a relatively short amount of time.

The absolute golden rule to successful investments is making sure you don't put all your eggs in one basket. This means that you should resort to a variety of types of investments in a variety of businesses and industries.

The remainder of this book is dedicated to helping you find those precise dividend investment options that provide you with all the advantages with the least of the disadvantages as possible. Of course, it is impossible to predict the future - but even so, there are certain strategies you can use to minimize the risk of your dividend investments and maximize their profitability.

The Fundamental Rules of Dividend Investing

Dividend investing is not rocket science - it might feel confusing and downright anxiety-inducing when you first get into it, but it is still one of the easier investment methods to understand.

While these are not even by far the *only* rules of successful dividend investing, the fundamentals rely on analyzing the quality of the dividend-paying companies you invest in and in making sure that you have a long-term mindset in place when you start your investment journey into the world of dividends.

I will expand a little more on this on this chapter, to help you fully understand why these two laws of dividend investing are so crucial and why they should lie at the basis of every decision you will make from here on in terms of investments in dividends.

Quality

The quality of the company you want to buy stock in is extremely important because it will determine the actual quality of the stock itself (and thus, the profitability of the stock as well).

Not all stocks are created alike - some have higher yields, which makes them attractive for income investors, while others have lower yields but dividend potential, which makes them more appealing for value investors.

In general, a stock is considered to have a high dividend yield if it has a yield higher than that of the U.S. 10-Year Treasury (which was of 2.91% in 2018). [5]

---

[5] https://www.macrotrends.net/2016/10-year-treasury-bond-rate-yield-chart

However, just because a company's current dividend yield is higher than the aforementioned value, it does not necessarily mean that you should invest right away. To determine if a company is worth investing in for dividends, you should analyze whether or not their current yield is sustainable in the long run.

There are four ratios you should consider when running this analysis: the Dividend Payout Ratio, the Dividend Coverage Ratio, the Free Cash Flow to Equity Ratio, and the Net Debt to EBITDA Ratio. All of them will be discussed in more detail over the next chapter, where I will show you how to pick the best stocks for your dividend investing plan.

Long-Term Thinking

The Wolf of Wall Street is, undoubtedly, one of the best movies created around the world of investments, precisely because it manages to make stock shares *exciting*.

However, most of the real-life investment stories are far less glamorous than the story of Jordan Belfort (or his clients, for that matter). And dividend investing is as far from that as it can be.

Dividend investing is not where luxurious yachts and expensive watches lie - but it is where genuine realism and manageable expectations live.

If you are looking for a get-rich-quick-scheme, dividend investing is not where you should put your energy.

Dividend investing is for the long-term thinkers. For those of you want to celebrate retirement in peace, enjoying the finest of what life truly has to offer: the comfort of not worrying about money when you stop working, the ability to afford nice vacations and spoil your grandchildren every now and again.

It sounds a bit less glamorous than partying and living the luxury life - but it is a far more approachable dream, one every common person can actually attain.

When you start to get more in-depth with your know-how in the world of dividend investments, you will realize that the excitement comes in building portfolios that are bound to work, one way or another. The risks are there, same as with any other type of investment, but even so, dividend investing tends to be a far more secure way to multiply your money over the course of the years.

Yes, it might take decades for your dividend payments to actually amount to something considerable. But, while growth investment might be a lot about luck and striking more or less accidental gold, value investing is all about working with real data and predictions that don't fail under normal market circumstances.

What does that mean?

It basically means that, if your chosen dividend-paying company (or companies) continue on the same path as until now, it is more than likely that you will live a comfortable life in retirement. Given that the most recommendable companies for dividend investing have been around for quite some time, the worst things that could happen are huge market crashes, or major changes in economy, politics, and society.

For instance, if you choose to invest in General Motors, things are pretty much predictable. If people continue to use cars in the next decades (which is very likely they *will* do), your chosen company will continue more or less on the same path as before. Consequently, you will most probably continue to see dividend payments from them.

Predictability is not frequently associated with excitement - but when predictability means that you can afford to dream of a nice, comfortable life, it can be absolutely exciting.

Putting all your money in growth investments to sell the stock when prices rise sounds like the best idea for those of you who want to amass a fortune in a quick amount of time. However, if you remember the old story with the hare and the tortoise, you will also remember that *slow and steady wins the race*.

Of course, you should definitely diversify your portfolio as much as possible - but a long-term approach will help you make better choices not just for value investing, but also for growth options, precisely because it will help you temper down any impulsive, high-risk decisions.

Yes, dividend investing is worth it for a lot of reasons - and your own future is one of the single most important ones.

The next chapters are all about making the best choices for a financially healthy, steady future. A future that will not be turned upside down by the passing of a CEO or by the sudden apparition of a brand-new technology that disrupts the latest Silicon Valley Unicorn.

A future you can rely on.

How to Pick Stocks

In order for dividend investing to work, you first need to make sure you select the best stocks, and that you do it at the best moment.

There is no secret recipe to picking successful dividend-paying stocks, but there are a few things that will make the process easier and more reliable, leading to decisions that are more likely to be profitable in the long run.

What Is a "Quality" Company?

This question can be answered in a thousand and one ways. A quality company can be a company that brings value to its customers and to the market. It might be a company that is showing constant growth. Or it might simply be a company that has a proven track record of success in whatever endeavors they engaged in.

It all depends on where you stand and the lens you use to look at this question. If you have to filter this matter through the most important aspect of dividend investing (long-term reliability), a quality company will usually meet a cumulus of characteristics.

In theory, it's all very easy: you need a company that *does* pay dividends and then reinvests those dividends over the years so that you increase your net worth.

However, the quality of the company you are investing is can make or break this simple plan. Otherwise, you might have to face severe cuts in dividend payments, the complete elimination of these payments, or simply stock price depreciation.

The most important characteristics of a good company for dividend investing include the following:

Dividend Investing

1. Consistent profits. If a company records amazing profits one year and drops well below that the next year, it's a clear sign that it might not be the steadiest business.

2. Growth. As it was mentioned before, the best dividend paying companies are not growing at a staggering rate - but they are steady in the way they do this. This is quite important because you want to invest in dividend stocks that will appreciate over time. In general, look for businesses that show growth expectations that range between 5% and somewhere around 15%. Anything above that might lead to severe disappointments that will eventually hurt your portfolio's performance.

3. Good cash flow. Earnings are one thing, and cash flow is a completely different matter. The first will show you if a company is doing a good job, but the second will actually tell you whether or not that company will actually pay its dividends.

4. History. Generally, you should look for businesses that have increased their dividend payments over the past 5 years (or more). This will make it more

likely that your chosen company will increase their dividend payments over the next years as well.

5. The ex-dividend dates. This is quite significant because buying shares after this date means that you will not be eligible for the current round of dividend payments.

6. Debt. Most companies have some form of debt, but you should definitely stay away from those that show excessive debt. As you will see later on, there is a special ratio that should be calculated to help you determine just how indebted a company is. Most of the times, companies with a debt to equity ratio of more than 2 are to be avoided.

7. Industry. This is a characteristic that is frequently overlooked, but you shouldn't make the same mistake. For instance, investing in an oil company might not be the best option, precisely because the entire industry is hanging by a string. With oil reserves running low and new technologies pushing electric cars further (both in terms of performance and in terms of pricing), oil companies might soon find themselves struggling. It might not happen

overnight, but it is more than likely that they will not continue to grow any further.

8. At the same time, the healthcare industry is likely to boom over the next years. Not only are more and more discoveries made, but with the very numerous Baby Boomer generation aging, it is very probable that health services will be in higher demand over the next decades.

   Low CAPEX (Capital Expenditure). Companies with lower capital expenditure are past the phase where they need to constantly reinvest their profits for further growth. Consequently, this means that they are more probable to pay dividends, rather than reinvest their earnings entirely.

   This should be put into perspective a little. Some industries (like tech) need constant improvement and growth, so it should be a generally bad sign that a tech company is investing a very small percentage of their earnings into further research and growth.

   At the same time, companies like this are unlikely to pay dividends anyway, so you might as well avoid them altogether. A decent CAPEX is OK for dividend investing, but if most of the company's earnings are going into reinvestments, it is best to just move on to another option.

The Step by Step Process to Choosing the Right Stock

There is no such thing as a perfect recipe to help you choose the right stocks. There are, however, some steps you might want to consider before making the final purchase. Keep in mind that these steps will not necessarily lead you to dividend investment success - more than that, they will help you find your own way in the world of investing and make the choices that are right for *you*.

Consider Your Goals

Every investor has their own reasons. Some people invest for retirement; others are simply looking to add more income to their current lives. Some want to save their money, and others want to strike gold by speculating a large gain. Everyone is different - and that is OK.

You need to decide where you stand on this spectrum and what your investment goals are. This will dictate a number of decisions down the road, including whether you want to focus more on growth investment (buying and selling stocks, for example) or income investing (dividends, for example).

Learn the Basics

You can't be successful at investing without learning the absolute basics. Yes, you cannot become a specialist overnight (and thus, your earnings will not be staggering either), but jumping headfirst without having learned the essentials behind investments is a very bad idea.

For example, some of the terms you will have to familiarize yourself with include: P/E ratio (the price-to-earnings ratio, which indicates how expensive a stock is or isn't), revenue growth (how much the sales of a company have gone up), and dividend yield (the percentage of the stock price that will be paid back to investors in the form of dividends).

This is far from everything you need to know. The world of investments is an intricate and complex affair. Thus, before you invest in stocks, bonds, or any other opportunities, you should first invest in your education. Understanding how everything works will move your investments well past the point of guesswork and into mathematical, logical, and business predictability.

Start with an Industry that Is Familiar to You

This will make things much easier for you because it will be much easier for you to understand how an investment works when it's applied to an industry you know.

It can be anything, really. In love with fairytale movies? You can always invest in Disney. Passionate about engineering? There are so many companies in this sector you can start your investment journey with!

This step is very important for two main reasons: it will provide you with a smooth introduction in the world of investing, and it will also help you keep your interest high (which is crucial, especially when you are just starting out and the odds of "dropping out" is higher).

As you grow more accustomed to investments and how they really function, you should start to spread your wings into other industries and sectors as well. Diversification is of the utmost importance for your success, so do make sure you step out of your comfort zone at some point, when you feel that you are ready to take on new realms.

Start Working It Out

Obviously, you shouldn't invest large sums of money at first, while you are just learning the ropes. Use your first experiments to bring together your interest in your chosen sector and your acquired knowledge. Analyze stocks from every point of view: the company offering them, the P/E ratio, the yield, the risks, and so on. And when you collect enough information to prove to yourself that a stock option is good for your portfolio, jump in and buy.

Remember that this process should be relatively fast. The more you wait, the more likely it is that the stock price will go up, which will ultimately diminish your investment's profitability in the long run.

The Main Ratios to Calculate

As I was mentioning a little earlier, there are four main calculations you should make to determine whether or not a company is worth investing in for its dividend payments. These calculations are as follows:

1. The Dividend Payout Ratio

To calculate this ratio, you should divide the annual dividends/ share by the earnings per share. This ratio will show you how much of a company's annual earnings/ share is paid in the form of cash dividends/ share.

It might seem that the more a company pays in dividends, the better it will be for you. However, keep in mind that the long-term game is what you are in for - and it is highly likely that a company that pays high dividends will not be able to sustain this over the next years or decades. Furthermore, a company that pays too much will not raise its dividend payments over the years - and, combined with inflation issues, this can lead to reduced profitability for you as an investor.

Generally speaking, if a company is paying less than half of its earnings as cash dividends is safe, and it should be considered quite stable.

2. The Dividend Coverage Ratio

To calculate this ratio, you should divide a company's yearly EPS (Earnings per Share) by its DPS (Dividends per Share).

This ratio will show you the number of times a business will be able to make dividend payments to common shareholders.

3. The Free Cash Flow to Equity Ratio

To calculate this ratio, you should determine the net income of a company and subtract the net capital expenditures, the potential debt repayments, and the changes that occur in net working capital. This will lead you to the amount of cash the company will be able to pay to its shareholders after all the expenses (and debts, when this is the case) have been paid.

While both the Dividend Coverage Ratio and the Dividend Payout Ratio are very important when it comes to determining a company's dividend investment quality, it is also very important to consider the Free Cash Flow to Equity Ratio because this will reveal just how much you might receive in the form of a cash dividend payment.

4. The Net Debt to EBITDA Ratio

Last, but definitely not least, you should also calculate the Net Debt to EBITDA ratio. To do this, divide the business' total liability (debt) by its EBITDA (Earnings before Interest, Taxes, Depreciation, and Amortization).

This ratio will show you a company's leverage and how able it is to meet its debt. Once you determine this ratio, you should compare it to industry averages because the actual percentage might vary a lot from one industry to another. The lower the ratio is, the more desirable it is that you invest in that company. The higher this ratio is, the more likely it is that this company will stop paying dividends in the future.

The Dividend Growth

Although not a ratio per se, the dividend growth is an important calculation you should make when deciding whether you should invest in a particular stock option or not.

The dividend growth rate is the percentile rate at which a stock's dividends grow over a period of time, on an annual basis.

To calculate the dividend growth rate, first determine the period of time you want to analyze. Take the value of the dividend at the end of that time span and divide it by its value at the beginning. Consider "N" to be the number of years in the time span you are analyzing and take the Nth root of the value you have calculated before. The resulting number will be your dividend growth rate.

Let's say that you are analyzing Apple stocks from 2015 to 2019. The dividend value at the beginning of this period is $0.10, and the dividend value at its end is $0.20. Dividing the latter value by the first results in "2". The fourth root of 2 is 1.18 - which is the dividend growth rate in this fictional example.

The Main Types of Dividend Stocks

In order for you to fully understand the kind of stocks you should be looking into and to make the best choice for your portfolio, it is quite important that you are familiar with the main types of dividend stocks.

In essence, they are all very similar - but they show significant differences you should be well aware of before buying any shares.

There are three main categories of dividend stocks: ADRs, MLPs, and REITs. Following, we will get into a more in-depth explanation of each and why you should (or shouldn't) invest in it.

ADRs

ADRs, short for American Depository Receipts, are an increasingly popular dividend investment option, as a lot of investors are focusing on foreign equity markets.

American Depository Receipts are a form of investment that allows investors to add foreign equity markets to their portfolios without investing in international mutual funds or buying foreign stock on foreign markets. Put simply, an ADR is a share you buy in a foreign company by using an American stock exchange (Nasdaq, the New York Stock Exchange, etc.). These stocks come in the form of negotiable certificates that are issued by a U.S. bank, representing the shares you purchase in your chosen foreign company.

One of the most common examples of foreign companies that allow you to purchase stock in their business includes Unilever, based in London, UK. This company has a very high trading volume of ADRs (one of the highest ever recorded, actually).

ADRs tend to rise in popularity in a time of political and economic uncertainty, precisely because they protect investor portfolios from the uncertainty of what is happening on American grounds.

The structure of an ADR is quite unique because U.S.-listed companies are usually backed by external company shares, which are held in trust by an American bank. The ADR shares in a company may have a 1:1 ratio (such as in the case of Unilever, for example), but this is rather rare (as Unilever is one of the companies with a high number of ADRs in their structure).

When dividend payments are issued by a foreign company with ADR shares in their structure, the U.S. bank holding these funds will collect these dividends in that country's currency, and then convert them into U.S. dollars. This means that you will not actually what your dividend payment is until you receive it, due to different currency fluctuations.

Moreover, you should know that these dividends are subjected to taxes withheld before the payment is actually processed. In most of these cases, however, you can claim a tax credit if your ADR shares are connected to a taxable account.

There are multiple advantages to holding ADR stocks in your portfolio. Some of the most important ones include:

- The fact that you can diversify your portfolio into foreign stock. This will help you create a well-rounded portfolio that poses as little risk as possible.
- You can make investments in U.S. dollars, rather than foreign currency (which would make you lose money on the currency exchange rate fluctuations not only when receiving the payments, but also when buying the stock itself).
- ADR shares are one of the single most convenient ways to invest in foreign stock and diversify your portfolio outside of the country. While it may not be the only foreign investment solution, it is by far one of the easiest to handle.
- When favorable currency fluctuations happen, you can capitalize on this as an investor, maximizing your stock's profitability

MLPs

MLP is short for Master Limited Partnership, and this type of investment has grown in popularity since the financial crisis of 2008. The reason they have become more popular for investors is because this type of dividend investing can yield attractive profits while being associated with a series of tax benefits.

Since the times of very low-interest rates are slowly coming to an end, and the economy has jumped back from the crisis it met in 2008, investors should now run a thorough comparison on whether MLPs make a better choice than traditional dividend stocks.

In very simple terms, MLPs are businesses that exist as publicly traded limited partnerships. Therefore, they have the tax advantages of a partnership and the advantageous liquidity of a public enterprise. This means that as an investor, you will be taxed only when the profits of the company are distributed.

There are two main types of MLP partners: limited partner investors (who usually buy shares in the company and then provide capital for the operations of the company) and general partner owners (who are also responsible with the management of the daily operations of the company).

It can be fairly said that MLPS are quite different than any kind of traditional dividends - but even so, when it comes to their profitability, they are closer to this category than any other.

MLPs are usually related to the energy industry, and they are traded on national exchanges. The reason these types of investments are focused on this very specific sector of the economy is because they were originally mandated to help energy companies manage the natural resources (this happened in the 1980s).

One of the defining differences between MLPs and traditional dividend stocks is consisted of the fact that the first is usually operated as pass-through entities. This means that they pass on cash and they do not have to pay corporate taxes. In most cases, this also means that an MLP will not retain a high percentage of their earnings to reinvest in the business.

MLPs have a structure that allows these partnership companies to raise capital from investors who qualify. Therefore, most of the cash flow of an MLP is used for the payouts. In the case of a dividend stock in the traditional sense of the term, this is not the case because payouts are to be determined by a company's dividend per share ratio.

Furthermore, participation in a traditional dividend paying company is a lot more limited than in the case of an MLP. At the same time, dividend-paying companies pertain to a wider range of sectors and industries than MLPs which, as mentioned above, are usually connected to the energy sector.

Do note that even though an MLP is a pass-through entity, the dividend earnings are still taxed as any other type of ordinary income (at a lower rate than normally most of the times, but they are not completely exempt of income tax).

REITs

In a nutshell, a REIT (Real Estate Investment Trust) is a type of security that behaves like normal stock in terms of trading but is mainly focused on the real estate market.

The vast majority of the REITs are centered on property ownership and rentals, but some are also connected to financing properties and mortgages. These real estate investment trusts were born in 1960 when Congress decided to offer small and large investors the chance to reap the benefits of the real estate profits. There are several regulations REITs must abide by (such as a minimum of 100 shareholders and having at least 75% of their assets and income active in the real estate industry).

The companies issuing a REIT are active (for the most part) in the real estate industry, acting as property owners and landlords. REITs do not have an income tax obligation at the corporate level, which makes this form of legal organization advantageous for its owners.

In the case of a REIT, the tax obligation is passed to the individual investors - but in return, the company will pay them at least 90% of the earnings as dividends. This means that this type of investment can result in a very high yield.

Since REIT dividends are not qualified for the capital gains rate of 15%, they are taxed as usual, as per the investor's normal income tax rate.

If you decide to invest in REITs, you should do it via major brokers, just as you would do with any other type of stock.

Stock Selection Strategies and Building a Portfolio

As I was mentioning in a previous chapter, the two main rules of dividend investing are paying attention to the quality of a company and making sure you think with the long-term plan in mind.

Building an investment portfolio is all about creating diversity, which will maximize your gains and minimize the risks at the same time. Dividend investing should be a part of this portfolio, especially if you decide to invest for retirement or for another long-term goal.

Selecting the right stocks to add to your portfolio is, obviously, very important. Beyond the quality of the company offering dividend stocks, you should also consider a series of factors - such as the form by which these stocks are organized and the way they are paid out. This will help you create a more accurate prediction of your earnings in the future so that you know exactly what to expect.

There are four main subjects I would like to touch on here: ETFs, DRIPs, dividend capture strategies, and the so-called Dogs of the DOW. These are some of the main methods you can choose from when making dividend investments, and it is very important that you understand how they work so that you can create the right mix of them for your investment portfolio.

So, without further ado, let's dive into this.

ETF

ETFs (Exchange-Traded Funds) are listed and traded on a stock exchange - meaning that most of the times, they "behave" just like any other type of stock: they are purchased through a broker, and the profits are filtered through that broker as well.

When you invest in an ETF, your money will be brought together with the money of the other investors and the company will invest the collective sum according to their declared objective.

Most of the times, ETFs aim to produce returns that either track or replicate a very specific type of index - like the stock index or the commodity index, for example.

These ETFs are usually managed passively by Exchange-Traded Funds managers, and they do not usually outperform the index they are tracking (they do not aim to do that). Therefore, ETFs that track indexes are usually associated with lower fees and charges than investment funds.

There are multiple types of ETFs, categorized according to their structure (e.g., cash-based ETFs vs. synthetic ETFs). Furthermore, many ETFs are considered to be Specified Investment Products (SIPs), which means that you may or may not qualify to make an investment of this kind.

ETFs can yield profit in two main ways: by capital gains (when the price of the units you purchased in said ETFs rises above their purchase price) and by receiving dividends.

One of the major disadvantages of ETFs is connected to the fact that they do not guarantee your principal. So, for example, if you invest $50,000 in an ETF and the company fails, you will not only not profit from this investment, but you might lose the invested money as well. These risks are usually highlighted in the prospectus, so you should pay a lot of attention to every piece of information you receive.

Obviously, there are a lot of advantages for ETF investments as well. Some of the most popular ones include:

- The fact that you can actually gain exposure to indexes and their performance without investing in all of their component stocks.
- The fees and the charges are usually smaller than those of actively managed funds.
- Most often, there is no sale charge associated with ETFs.

Do keep in mind the fact that ETFs might not be for everyone. To make this type of investment, you should make sure you:

- Want potentially high profits, but at the same time, you are ready to face potential variable returns and losing all (or a large chunk) of your initial investment.
- Understand very precisely how ETF returns are calculated, as well as the factors that might affect these calculations.
- Understand that your money will be blocked for a long period of time.
- You are prepared to make a long-term investment, as this is one of the safest ways to ensure that short-term price fluctuations will not affect your business. Some ETFs might be suitable for more short-term investments, but this is a matter that needs to be thoroughly analyzed.
- You are fairly familiar with both the ETF's track record and with the manager handling it.

Aside from the major advantages and disadvantages, you should also consider the main types of ETFs, so that you know which one(s) suit your objectives the best. Do note that these ETF categories are created based on their structure, and not necessarily the underlying index they are tracking (two ETFs can track the same index and be structured differently).

The main types of ETFs are the following:

1. Cash-based. This ETFs are invested directly into an index's assets as follows:
   - The entirety of that index's component bonds, assets, or stocks
   - A part of the index's component bonds, assets, or stocks.

2. Synthetic. These ETFs are slightly more complex than cash-based ETFs because they use derivative products - such as access products or swaps to produce returns.

   Put in very simple terms, this means that more parties will be involved in an ETF's derivative products (e.g., the counterparty of the swap or the issuer of the access product).

   This comes with risks you should be aware of. For instance, if the other party involved in a derivative product defaults on their payment obligations, you might end up losing a substantial amount of money (depending on how much the ETF is exposed to the other party).

DRIP

DRIPs (or Dividend Reinvestment Plans) are programs that give investors the opportunity to reinvest their dividends into buying more stock in the company. Sometimes, this term is used to refer to an automatic reinvestment arrangement you have with your brokerage company, but most of the times, DRIP is a formal program created by a publicly traded corporation which is available to its already existing shareholders.

It is quite easy to understand how these plans work. Normally, when dividend payment is issued, the shareholders will receive a check deposited directly into their bank account. With a DRIP program, you can use the money to reinvest it in additional shares, purchased directly from the company (as opposed to buying them from the stock market, using the services of a brokerage agency). This means that no commission fees will be applied for the transaction, and the redemption of the shares happens directly between you and that company as well.

DO keep in mind the fact that even though you will not receive the actual dividends, you still have to report this as taxable income. Exceptions from this rule make situations when these dividends are held in tax-benefited accounts, such as IRAs.

Dividend Reinvestment Plans show both advantages and disadvantages - and you should be aware of both in order to make the best decision.

The main advantages of a DRIP program include the following:

- The opportunity to buy stock at a discounted price (which can be as high as 10% of the current stock price).
- The opportunity to not pay commission fees
- The possibility to buy fractional shares
- The automatic nature of the program and its long-term profitability. The more time you spend in a DRIP, the more shares you will continue to receive, and thus, by the end of the cycle, you will own a considerable amount of shares in that company, which you can monetize in different ways.

The main disadvantages of a DRIP program, on the other hand, include the following:
- The shares are not liquid
- The dividends will still be taxed
- You aren't given with a choice

Dividend Capture Strategy

There are several strategies you can employ when building your dividend portfolio - but the dividend capture one is, by far, one of the more popular (and exciting) options you have. The dividend capture strategy tends to be more popular with day traders (who buy stock and sell it by the end of the day). This strategy involves the frequent buying and selling of stocks and holding them for short amounts of time (enough for you to capture the dividend payment on the stock).

This strategy is not necessarily geared at long-term investors who are ready to wait for long periods of time to see their yields. Instead, this strategy is aimed at shorter-termed gains, and it focuses on dividends that are paid monthly (they are less common than annual or quarterly dividends, but they do exist).

A typical dividend capture strategy timeline includes four main points:

- The declaration date (the date at which the company declares its dividends, which is usually in advance of the payment by a lot).
- The ex-dividend date (the date at which new shareholders stop being eligible to receive the dividend payment and the date at which the stock price will most likely drop, depending on the declared dividend amount).
- The date of record (the last date shareholders are eligible to receive the dividend payments).
- The pay date (the actual date when the dividends are released to their shareholders)

One of the main traits that make this strategy so attractive to so many investors is the fact that it is *simple*. You don't need to run in-depth, fundamental analyses on anything, and you do not need to chart anything either. In very simplistic terms, what you need to do is purchase stock shares before the ex-dividend date and sell them after that. If the price per share drops (which might happen), all you have to do is wait until it comes back to its initial value.

Furthermore, you do not necessarily need to hold the stock until the pay date (provided that the stock price will come back by then, of course).

In an ideal world where stock markets are operated according to perfect mathematical logic, this strategy would not work - but alas, markets don't function according to perfect rules.

For instance, if you buy a share worth $10 before the ex-dividend date, if the dividend is worth $0.5, and if you sell your share with $9.75 after the ex-dividend rate, you will make a $0.25 in profit. That does not seem like much - but multiply this by the hundreds, and you will see how the dividend capture strategy can yield attractive profits in a very short amount of time (sometimes, as short as one day). Moreover, when you do this every day (because almost every day in the calendar offers a dividend paying stock), you will be able to reap considerable benefits.

If you decide to use the dividend capture strategy to maximize your return, you should also be aware of the tax implications that come with this. More specifically, due to the short-term nature of these investments, you will most likely have to pay your normal income tax for these profits (as opposed to the preferential tax rates applied for qualified dividends, and which are taxed at 20%, 15%, or as low as 0%).

Taxes can be a deterrent for those of you considering the dividend capture strategy - but, again, do keep in mind that doing this in an IRA trading account might help you avoid the taxes on dividends.

It is also important to know that some transaction costs might be applied in the case of dividend captures as well, minimizing the gains even more. However, it is also essential to note that there are some risks associated with this method as well:

- If the price of the stock drops on the ex-date by more than the amount of the dividend, you will have to maintain your stocks for a longer period of time than you initially planned, to make sure the price gets back up to its initial value.

- Unfortunate and impermissible market movements can also affect your gains when using the dividend capture strategy. This risk can be somewhat minimized if you only focus on blue-chip companies (businesses that have a national reputation for being extremely reliable and show the ability to make profits in both goods times and bad times).

Dogs of the Dow

The Dogs of the Dow strategy is quite popular, and, as you will see, there are several good reasons that make it so appreciated by a wide range of investors.

This strategy involves investments that use the 10-highest dividend stocks on the Dow Jones Industrial Average index every year. These dividend stocks are offered by blue-chip companies, and they are qualified as a high dividend by one of the oldest, most reliable, and popular indexes in the world.

One of the main advantages of the Dogs of the Dow strategy is connected precisely to the fact that investments made in such companies are quite predictable - so they will more or less fall in line with your plans.

This entire strategy relies on the assumption that blue-chip companies will not change their dividends based on the trading conditions of any kind. Therefore, their dividends are frequently considered to show the worth of the company.

While stock prices for these businesses may fluctuate over the course of a business cycle - the higher the dividends, the more the price will increase towards the end of the business cycle. This means that reinvesting in this type of companies every year will help you outperform the overall market.

There are 30 companies comprising the Dow Jones Industrial Average, and all of them pay dividends. Moreover, as blue-chip companies, they are considered to be highly reliable even if market changes affect other companies' profitability.

The Dogs of the Dow strategy is not about investing in all of the Dow Jones companies - but in those that show the best yields per share. These dividend yields can be as high 5.7% (such as in the case of IBM in 2019), but they do not generally drop below 2.9% (such as in the case of Merck & Co. in 2019). [6]

The main idea behind the Dogs of the Dow investment strategy is to pick easy and safe stocks. Ideally, you should do this on the last day of the year, after the stock market closes, by looking at the highest yielding stocks on the Dow

---

[6] https://www.forbes.com/sites/investor/2019/01/02/the-8-dogs-of-the-dow-for-2019-include-replacements-cisco-systems-and-jpmorgan/#252bb3a5200e

index. On the first day of the next year, you should invest an equal amount of money in all of the selected stocks, and then hold the portfolio for approximately one year.

There are a lot of tools to help you make the best choices when it comes to the Dogs of the Dow options - including opinion pieces, forecasts, calculators, and so on. It is important to study all of these to make sure you are fully informed and that the stocks you are buying are the best options for your portfolio.

The Dogs of the Dow strategy is not for the short-distance runners, but for the long-term strategists. While the Dogs of the Dow sometimes outperform the Dow, this is not mandatory. The key here is investing long term and maximizing on the good years by creating an average over time that will provide you with the best profitability in the long run.

Of course, these are just four of the main strategies associated with dividend investing - and while they are most definitely among the most popular, it is still quite important that you do your own research. The more accustomed you get with the world of dividend investing, the more complex your strategies and portfolio will become, helping you reap all the benefits this form of investment has to offer and downplay the less advantageous sides.

Following, I will present you with some of the most important tips to know when it comes to protecting your investments and ensuring you don't make major mistakes along the way. Following this advice will help you stay as far away as possible from the potential risks of investments (particularly, from the risks of dividend investments) so that you can make the most out of your portfolio even if parts of it do not perform as well as they should be.

Protecting Your Investments

Building a profitable portfolio is as much about selecting the right stocks as it is about making sure you take care of them. Protecting your investments is essential if you want them to be profitable for the long run. While you may not be able to predict the future and you most likely do not hold an Artificial Intelligence smart enough to be able to make all the predictions for you, there are still a lot of things you can do to ensure the safety and longevity of your portfolio.

This chapter is dedicated entirely to this: helping you understand how important investment protection is and what are the main things you can do to keep your portfolio profitable.

Diversifying

Diversifying your portfolio is the single most important thing you should do to make sure it will stay profitable over the years. The more diverse your portfolio is, the more likely it is that even if one or two elements of it do not perform well, you will still be able to reap benefits from your investments. For instance, if the market drops, a diverse portfolio will make it less likely that you lose all your assets. One of the most relevant examples to give here is the economic crisis of 2008 when many investors saw their returns diminished partially and even totally. Those with diverse portfolios, however, managed to survive the crisis better than those who had invested in mostly the same type of stocks, for the same companies.

Mere diversification will not help much, though. It is quite important to know what type of investments to make, how much to invest in each of them, and how to make sure you are smart about the diversification itself.

Some of the essential rules to follow when diversifying your investment portfolio include the following:

Variety over Quantity

Having a diverse portfolio is not about quantity, but about a wider variety of investment categories. Ideally, you should strive for all of the major types of investments:

- Stocks to help you grow your portfolio;
- Real estate funds to protect your investments from stock market falls. In general, real estate investments are less prone to be affected by inflation fluctuations;
- International securities are very important, given the high level of globalization (and the fact that expanding into other markets will provide you with opportunities to grow your portfolio);
- Cash to give your investment portfolio some stability and security;
- Bonds to provide you with income

Split Your Money Correctly

No matter how much money you can invest right now, it is quite important to know how to allocate it correctly.

One of the first things you should do is set up some money in both cash and income investments. This will help you with potential emergencies and short-term goals (or, in other words, it will help you "save for the rainy days").

Furthermore, there are many rules you can follow when it comes to splitting your investments. One of the most popular ones is to subtract your current age from 100 and use the result to determine the percentage of stocks to invest in. The remainder will be invested in stocks. For instance, if you are 30, you should put 70% in stocks and 30% in bonds. Keep in mind that you might want to do this through a 401k plan or IRA plan, as taxes will be more advantageous for you this way.

Next, you want to make sure you diversify both your stock investments and your bonds. One way to do this is by following this pattern:

- 10% to 25% should go in international securities (determine just how high the percentage of this will be based on your age and affluence - the younger and more affluent you are, the more you should invest in international securities);

- Take an equal amount of money from what you set aside for your stock portfolio and for your bonds and invest them in REITs. Ideally, this should be at around 10% of the total investment sum. Although real estate securities can be more volatile than other types of investments, they can also yield impressive returns, so it is worth putting at least a smaller part of your investment in this category.

- Make sure you split your investments when it comes to the types of stocks as well. Mutual funds tend to be attractive because you will not have to pay trading fees every time you invest in new stock. However, you should only invest part of your money in mutual funds - dividends and growth stock should be on your list as well. This way, even if your mutual fund fails or doesn't yield the expected results, you will still have money in other places (and you will not lose it all on one bet).

Keep in mind that diversification comes with a price, as well. Namely, a diverse portfolio might slice your annual returns, precisely because financial markets rely a lot on the risk and reward cycle. So, the less you risk, the less you win, and the more you risk, the more potential for great gains you have, This is *not* to say that you should play the stock market like you would play poker. Investments are far from gambling! There is a certain amount of luck involved in not knowing with 100% certainty what will happen to a company or a market in the next two, three, or thirty years. Even so, you should only make informed decisions and diversify your investments to a point where you protect yourself from tremendous losses.

In the end, only you can decide just how much you invest in riskier options and how much you invest in options that are safer. The rule where you subtract your age from 100 may or may not work for you, depending on your age, on the amount of money you can afford investing right now, as well as how much risk you want to take (and how much would keep you awake at night).

I highly recommend you talk to a professional about this. Every investor is different and aims for different yields, so a face to face discussion with someone who knows the ins and outs of the investment world will give you a clearer idea on where to put your money (and how).

Case in point is that diversification is utterly important. Say, for instance, that you have invested a large sum of money in an oil company and just a small amount in everything else.

With the rise of electric cars, however, oil will become less and less used - to the point where it will go completely extinct. Studies say that we have about 50 more years of oil left, so investing in this type of company is bound to attract losses on your portfolio, sooner or later.

However, putting your money in companies and industries that are more future-proof, safer, and more diverse will help you avoid facing the entirety of the negative effects that come with a market crash.

Are They Still Paying a Dividend?

As I was mentioning earlier in this book, whether or not a company pays its dividends is up to them. There is no legal bound to push them into doing this - they may do it, or they may not do it.

Sometimes, companies that used to pay dividends stop doing it. There is a myriad of reasons why they might choose to proceed this way: they might want to reinvest more, they might be facing market-related issues, or they may simply want to release a new product and reinvest all their earnings in that.

There is no way you can predict with absolute accuracy whether or not a business will continue to pay dividends. In general, blue-chip companies do this (and they are labeled this way precisely because they have great power on the market, and they can thrive in times of adversity as well). However, with most other companies, predictability is a pretty big issue.

Seeing dividend cuts can be a real nightmare for any investor. When you put your money in dividend stocks, you expect to see a certain amount of returns - but if dividend payments get cut, you might have to face the fact that your entire retirement plan has gone South.

One of the first things you should do to protect yourself from companies that will soon stop paying dividends is quite obvious: do your homework. Just because a business has been paying their dividends for the past few years, it doesn't mean that they will continue to do it. So, before investing, look for signs of potential financial trouble in that business, or simply for signs that they are looking to expand beyond their normal rate.

Another thing you might want to do is to simply go for the companies that have consistently grown their dividends over the past few years. Of course, this is not a guarantee that they will continue to grow their dividends or that they will continue to pay them, but it is a fairly good indicator.

Last, but not least, know that just because a company is very big and very popular, it does not automatically mean they pay dividends. You would be surprised, but some of the most famous businesses of the moment don't do it:

- Google may have ended the year with more than $100 billion in cash [7], but even so, they did not release any plans on paying dividends to its investors. Even more, most predictions point to the fact that Alphabet, the company owning Google, will continue to grow at a really high pace (by approximately 13% in earnings and 20% in the sale). At the same time, though, Google never pointed to a promise to pay

---

[7] https://edition.cnn.com/2019/02/04/investing/google-alphabet-cash-dividend/index.html

the dividends - they have continuously reiterated that they will not do this very soon.

- Amazon itself has not paid any dividends yet. However, some predictions say that they might soon be able to do this, as the business has reached full maturity, with more than $26 billion in cash flow. Until they make an official statement on the matter, though, this is all supposition, and you cannot rely on Amazon to pay dividends unless they clearly specify so. [8]

Keep Your Ears Open

Once you get used to their basics, financial markets and investments can be really fascinating. Yes, it's all charts and numbers and predictions - but beyond all of that, there are real businesses, with real struggles and real successes.

Staying in touch with the latest news in the field is extremely important because it will help you determine the right moment to buy stock, whether or not a company will pay dividends, or when you need to sell your stock.

---

[8] https://www.fool.com/investing/2019/01/14/will-2019-be-amazons-dividend-debut.aspx

Dividend Investing

Thankfully, the internet is full of sites and blogs you can read on a daily basis to make sure you stay on top of everything going on. However, it is quite essential that you base most of your decisions on well-established sources of information. As you may very well know it, anyone can release false rumors online and get away with it, so it's always best to back-trace your news to the major outlets out there.

Some of the most reliable sources of information for investors include:

MarketWatch News Viewer: global markets, stocks, Forex, commodities, asset classes, analyses of the macroeconomic data at country level, and so on.

Bloomberg: news categorized according to different areas of interest (such as region, industry, or asset class).

Reuters: stock specifics, market specifics, sector specifics, and so on.

The Wall Street Journal: global following for the financial news, for the price quotes, and so on. It also provides an email alert option based on your chosen criteria (so you can be instantly notified if they post anything about a company of interest, or any other area you might want to be fully in touch with). This is a paid source (so you can only see the headlines for free).

The Financial Times: similar to the aforementioned WSJ, also a paid source.

CNBC: global market news categorized according to region.

Of course, these are just some of the most important sources of information - many others can be used. As long as you double-check your tips with other sources as well, you will be able to rely on the information provided by most of the big sites on the internet.

Stop Losses

Stop loss is a technique mostly used by growth investors, but it can be applied to value investments as well. For stock traders, a stop loss is a limit they place on how much they can afford to lose - once that limit is reached, they will automatically stop making investments in a specific, predefined company or type of stock.

A similar strategy can and should be employed with dividend investing as well. Same as with playing poker, it is crucial that you know when to withdraw yourself from the game before you lose more than you can actually afford.

Some of the techniques you can use to stop losses when investing in stocks include the following:

- Place a limit order on buying. This will allow you to buy a stock when the price is at its lowest, not when the stock price is at its highest on the market (e.g., when everyone is talking about a particular stock). The limit order will be placed with your brokerage agency, and they will proceed to buy a certain amount of stock in a given company as soon as the price hits your preferred low mark.
- Place a limit order on selling. If you decide to sell your stock, you want to do it when the price is at its highest. Same as with buying limit orders, you can set selling limit orders as well and instruct your agent to sell your stocks when they reach a certain threshold.

Setting a stop loss is a debatable action for long-term investors. While it might make perfect sense for short term investors and traders, it might not for those who are in this for the long run.

More specifically, it is generally advised to wait for the stocks to come back because it will provide you with more benefits to keep them in your portfolio if they do. Even so, setting a more relaxed stop loss order on your stocks could help you make sure that its value will not be affected by an underperforming or failing stock that drops *too* much below the price at which you purchased it.

Panic and agitation are part of a trader's life (particularly, part of a day trader's life). But this might not be the case for dividend investors. If we had to compare the two, a trader or a short-term investor is more like coffee lovers who just need the caffeine "hit" and don't spend too much time savoring their drinks.

On the other hand, a long-term dividend investor will know how to sip their coffee, enjoy the aroma, and wait for the cloudy days to end. It is important to know when to stop waiting and admit that a company is failing entirely - but even so, you should not panic as soon as the stock prices drop.

The beauty of dividend investing is that you don't have to be connected to all the stock market news 24/7. You can move on to enjoy your life and make the most out of it while your portfolio is working for you, while constantly adding investments to it at your own pace and cadence.

The Most Common Mistakes to Avoid

Nobody is perfect, not even the most experienced investors on the market.

The great news is that you have decades and decades of dividend investment stories to look at and learn from so that you can avoid the mistakes of your "predecessors."

This chapter is all about avoiding the mistakes that could turn your dividend investing plan upside down in a relatively short amount of time. Most of the times, these mistakes are not so much related to the actual technique or strategy a new investor will employ, but to their mentality overall.

As I was saying towards the beginning of this book, dividend investing is not a race - it's a long-term marathon. Spinning out of control and racing before everyone else might be good in a competition that tests your speed, but it will be far from beneficial for a marathon, where resistance and long-term techniques matter more than anything.

Obviously, there are a thousand and one mishaps you can stumble across on your road to building a profitable portfolio. Following, I have gathered some of the most common ones, though - the ones you are likely to make when you are new in the game and want to do as much as possible in as little time as possible.

Chasing High Yields

Chasing high yields is perfectly fine - but when this becomes the sole goal of your entire investment strategy, you have a big problem to handle; you are not in the right competition. Dividend investments are not always about the highest yields (although adding some of them to your portfolio will surely help). It is also about the safest yields, the stocks that have the potential to grow in terms of dividend payments, and the investment options that will provide you with the best profit to risk ratio.

So, why are high yields not entirely desirable all the time? For once, they might also come with huge risks that are just not congruent with the philosophy of a long-term investor. Even more, the very high yield dividend stocks might also be associated with trouble. It may sound weird, but big profits are not always a sign of success, as they can be a sign of growth that goes at a pace that's too fast to be healthy.

The main takeaway here is to never buy stock just because it comes with a high yield. Sometimes, this yield might be associated with high dividend payments, but it might also be associated with a low price/ share (which might indicate company issues). Run a thorough analysis of the business you want to invest in and never go in this blindfolded - keep your eyes, your ears, and your mind open.

Furthermore, you should also try to focus more on current dividends, rather than future dividends. You cannot predict the future, but you can apply better management to your current dividends and make sure that they are well-protected.

Even more than that, keep in mind that even if a company has a high yield stock that is generated by actually high dividend payments, you should still stay informed. Even the biggest giants on the market can fail (such as in the case of Chrysler) - so it is essential to know when this happens so that you can take appropriate action.

Last, but definitely not least, some high yield stocks may be perceived this way because they are cheap. Buying stocks just because they are cheap is similar to buying the 100th pair of shoes just because it's on discount: you don't need it, you don't even desire it that much, it will take a considerable amount of space in your home, and the entire purchase will leave you without money and without the value that usually comes with well-strategized purchases.

Starting When You're Old

You may think you are young and that you are far from retirement - and truly, from where you are probably standing, the days of retired glory might seem centuries away.

However, the sooner you start with your long-term investments, the better off you will live during your retirement, precisely because your investments will have more time to mature and offer you the comfort you need once you stop being active on the workforce.

Every age comes with its own investment recommendations. They might be somewhat general, and they do not necessarily apply to each and every person, but keeping them in mind can help you a lot.

For instance:

1. If you are in your 30s, you have roughly 30-40 years for your investments to reach their full potential. In this case, even if the stock prices fall, your investments will not be hurt so much because your portfolio will have years (and even decades!) to recover.

    Some of the best places to start your investments in your 30s are your 401(k) and 403(b) accounts. The reason these accounts are so great? They are widely popular among employers who offer them to their workers, and they will usually come with tax exemptions (up to the moment of withdrawal, at least).

In general, you should try to invest approximately 10% to 15% of your current salary in these accounts. Doing this at a steady pace over the next decades will eventually help you retire safely.

A Roth IRA can also be a good option at this age, and one of its main advantages is that this account will come tax-free for its entire life cycle.

Stock funds and a smaller investment in bonds will also help you build a healthy portfolio starting with your 30s. If you want to take a bit more risk, investing about 70% of stock funds is a good idea. If, however, you want to be a bit safer, you can also consider mutual funds (these will ramp up when you are younger, and they will slowly start to become more conservative as you get near your retirement).

Last, but not least, real estate might also be a good investment. For instance, you might decide to buy your own house if you decide that you want to live in a certain location for at least five years. Investing in a rental property or a REIT fund can also work at this age too. Generally speaking, though, if you live in an overpriced market (such as New York City for example), real estate investments might not make much sense to you right now.

2. If you are in your 40s, you are already past the average age at which most people start making their first investments. However, there is still enough time for you to build a profitable portfolio.

   At this age, your 401(k) and 403(b) accounts can still provide you with a pretty good head start, as long as you invest the maximum you can. If you invest the upper limit of $18,000 in your 401(k), for example, you will have one million dollars by the time you retire. It may not be much if you take inflation into consideration, but even so, it is a more than generous starting point for your retirement funds.

   In general, if you are in your 40s, you want to build a portfolio that is slightly safer than the kind of portfolio you would be building in your 30s. Because you have less time before the actual retirement, you want to make sure that a market hit will not completely ruin your retirement dreams. Therefore, it is best for you now to invest in low-risk bonds and other types of fixed investments.

Do make sure to include international stock and REITs in your portfolio variety as well. This will help you stay safer and see better yields for your investments once you retire.

3. If you are in your 50s, it might be too late to *start* investing. Of course, you can still amass a considerable sum of money, but ideally, you should spend your 50s ramping up your current investments and doing the math to see how much money you will have by the time you retire (and how much of it you will owe in taxes).

They say age is but a number - but when it comes to investments, you want to start earlier, rather than later. The more time you have at your disposal, the larger the fortune you can amass, so that you can spend your retirement just as you want it: cruising through the rivers of Europe, raising your grandchildren, or simply living beautifully in a nice house.

Getting Bored

Truly, boredom must be the archenemy of everything produced in the world. It is boredom that pushes you to procrastinate scrolling down endless Facebook homepages, and it is boredom that pushes you away from the things that once made you feel passionate.

What this world needs is, perhaps, a little more stoicism to it (where "stoicism" is to be understood as the philosophical current based on withstanding adversity by the power of willpower and diligence).

The same goes for dividend investing as well.

Let's face it: dividend investing is not the roller coaster of Wall Street and it is more than likely that nobody will ever make a movie about it.

It is, however, one of the sanest, healthiest, and safest ways to ensure your investment portfolio has a solid foundation to it.

Yes, dividends might not feel as exciting as the adrenaline-inducing lives of day traders. But that doesn't mean that you should give up on them.

Boredom can very easily make you fall off the track with your long-term investments. One month can slip by, and then another one, and before you know it, you are in your mid-40s, trying to figure out what happened to your retirement plan.

Stick to your plan, be diligent about it, and make sure you don't let boredom deter you from your main course!

Following the Crowd

Following trends might be OK when it comes to fashion. But when it comes to investments, it is important to know that following the crowd is usually a bad idea.

Why?

Because the more attention a stock receives, the higher the price will be. So, unless you were the first in line and bought the stock back when it was still relatively unpopular, you should probably steer clear of anything that is too vocal in the financial media.

Deciding to buy stocks based on hot tips you receive from one source or another is an impulsive way to handle your investments, and it can lead to serious financial issues. While hot tips can definitely help you find the stocks worth investing in, you should still do your research and see if that "tip" follows up with data as well.

Otherwise, you are just gambling - and, as I was saying before, investing is not a game of poker, Blackjack, or roulette. It is a game that *needs* you to do your homework before anything else so that you can make the best and most informed decisions.

Conclusion

Dividend investing may not be as Hollywood-popular as day trading, but that doesn't make it *easy* in any way.

Same as with any type of investment, dividends need all of your undivided attention: they need you to *know* the ins and outs of how they work and the types of profits they can bring into your portfolio. But more than anything, dividends need you to treat them carefully: with the attention to detail of a bridal seamstress adjusting her daughter's dress for the Big Day.

Because they are generally considered to be a slightly safer option, dividend investments are also associated with *rush* decisions based on nothing more than scarce tips, choppy data, and a lack of understanding of how everything works, really.

My main goal with this book was to give you the tools to start your journey into the world of dividends: a world that might not shine bright like the diamonds of Wall Street, but which can shed light over your future and make it feel safer, comfier, and generally, *better*.

What I would really like to emphasize is that dividend investing should not be treated jokingly in any way. Because it generally shows small returns on each share, dividend investing is frequently considered petty or simply *not enough* - but the absolute truth is that using the right strategies will help you make pennies into fortunes.

This is not just an empty promise: dividend investing is part of most investors' portfolios precisely because it makes sense and it because it can provide you with a sense of security that lets you sleep well at night.

Don't get this the wrong way: when it comes to investments, nothing can ever be certain (and this is something I have emphasized throughout this book numerous times). But, compared to other forms of investing, dividends are fairly safer, especially when you play the game by their own rules. If day trading is all about seeing the light of the next day and making transactions that will eventually strike the golden pot at the end of a fairytale rainbow, dividends are all about *perspective* and long-term thinking.

Focusing solely on stock ownership or trading is never a good strategy - the economic crisis of 2008 has proved this quite well (as I have mentioned it before). Adding safer components to your portfolio will, however, help you create the future you want.

A future where your children have access to better education and a better chance at being successful in general.

A future where you finally have both the time and the money to go out and see the world and its marvels.

A future where you don't have to worry much because the work you have done in the last three decades to build a strong investment portfolio is finally paying off.

A future where you can wake up every day and smile, knowing that you don't have to work anymore, and don't have to feel anxious about your financials.

This is not to say that dividend investing is a magical key to living a happy life - but it can definitely help you build a stable, recurrent, healthy income that will lay the foundation of a better future for you and your loved ones.

Hopefully, my book has helped you put things in perspective, both when it comes to how dividends work and how to make the most out of them and when it comes to their role in an investment portfolio. More than that, I hope that my book has given you hope and a push of ambition. Dividend investing is not easy, but it's not rocket science either - and that makes it the perfect choice for those of you who are ready to put a bit of effort and see considerable results growing over the years.

If your portfolio were a cherry tree, I hope this book was the seed that helped you understand how to plan, grow, and maintain your tree to reap its fruits when the time comes.

Happy and safe investing ahead! Keep your head on your shoulders and your feet on the ground but keep your dreams beautiful and your hopes high too! It's the key to building the kind of future you deserve!

Leave a review

Reviews are one of the most important factors in a book's success. Even if you are a bestselling author, your new book - which you have toiled on for years - can have its chances of success ruined within a matter of moments by a few negative reviews (genuine or not).

It would mean so much to me if you would take a moment to visit the page (or any of my other titles) on a few of the major retailers and vote on the existing reviews (or place a review yourself).

If you don't wish to write a review, you can still help by simply voting Helpful or Unhelpful (or Thumbs up or Down) to the top 10 or so reviews. As always, please feel free to leave an honest review, whether positive or negative.

www.ingramcontent.com/pod-product-compliance
Lightning Source LLC
Chambersburg PA
CBHW072213170526
45158CB00002BA/588